Introduction to
Artificial intelligence
with Python

A Practical Learning Journey

Author

Paulo Fagundes

Foreword

Artificial Intelligence (AI) has radically transformed the way we interact with technology, solve complex problems, and understand data. This book is a practical guide for beginners who want to dive into the fascinating world of AI using Python, one of the most popular programming languages for developing intelligent systems.

Publisher

Shopline Business, *Brazil First Edition, 2024*

- **Category: Technical/Didactic Book**

Index

Introduction to Artificial Intelligence with Python

Summary

Chapter 1: Fundamentals of Artificial Intelligence

- Definition of Artificial Intelligence

- Brief history of AI
- Types of Artificial Intelligence
  - Weak AI
  - General AI (Strong AI)
  - Superintelligent AI

Chapter 2: Setting Up the Development Environment

Preparing Your Python Environment for AI

- Python Installation
- Essential Tools:
  - Anaconda
  - Jupyter Notebook
  - Google Colab
- Fundamental libraries:
  - NumPy
  - Pandas
  - Scikit-learn
  - TensorFlow
  - PyTorch

Configuration Code

```python
Python
# Installing the necessary libraries
!pip install numpy pandas scikit-learn tensorflow
matplotlib
```

Chapter 3: Machine Learning Fundamentals

Types of Machine Learning

1. Supervised Learning

2. Unsupervised Learning

3. Reinforcement Learning

Practical Example: Classification of Iris Flowers

```python
Python
from sklearn.datasets import load_iris
from sklearn.model_selection import train_test_split
from sklearn.neighbors import KNeighborsClassifier
from sklearn.metrics import accuracy_score

# Loading dataset
iris = load_iris()X, y = iris.data, iris.target

# Splitting data
X_treino, X_teste, y_treino, y_teste = train_test_split(X, y, test_size=0.3)

# Training
classifier model = KNeighborsClassifier(n_neighbors=3)
classifier.fit(X_treino, y_treino)

Python
from sklearn.datasets import load_iris
from sklearn.model_selection import train_test_split
from sklearn.neighbors import KNeighborsClassifier
from sklearn.metrics import accuracy_score

# Loading dataset
iris = load_iris()X, y = iris.data, iris.target

# Splitting data
X_treino, X_teste, y_treino, y_teste =
```

```
train_test_split(X, y, test_size=0.3)

# Training classifier model
 = KNeighborsClassifier(n_neighbors=3)
classifier.fit(X_treino, y_treino)

# Predicting prediction results
 = classifier.predict(X_teste)
accuracy = accuracy_score(y_teste,
predictions)print(f"Model accuracy: {accuracy *
100:.2f}%")

# Predicting predictions =
 classifier.predict(X_teste)
accuracy = accuracy_score(y_teste,
forecasts)print(f"Model Accuracy: {accuracy * 100:.2f}%")
```

Chapter 4: Neural Networks and Deep Learning

- Neural Network Basics

- Structure of an Artificial Neuron

- Frameworks de Deep Learning

- Simple Neural Network Example

Python

```
import tensorflow as tf
from tensorflow.keras.models import Sequential
from tensorflow.keras.layers import Dense

# Criando modelo de rede neural
modelo = Sequential([
    Dense(10, activation='relu', input_shape=(4,)),
    Dense(3, activation='softmax')
])

modelo.compile(optimizer='adam',
               loss='sparse_categorical_crossentropy',
               metrics=['accuracy'])

# Treinando o modelo
modelo.fit(X_treino, y_treino, epochs=50, verbose=0)
```

Chapter 5: Natural Language Processing (NLP)

- Introduction to NLP

- Basic techniques:

  o Tokenization

  o Text vectorization

- Sentiment Analysis Example

Python

```
from sklearn.feature_extraction.text import CountVectorizer
from sklearn.naive_bayes import MultinomialNB

# Exemplo simplificado de classificação de sentimento
textos = ["Adoro esse produto!", "Péssima experiência", "Mais ou menos"]
sentimentos = [1, 0, 2]  # positivo, negativo, neutro

vetorizador = CountVectorizer()
X = vetorizador.fit_transform(textos)

classificador = MultinomialNB()
classificador.fit(X, sentimentos)
```

Chapter 6: Ethics in Artificial Intelligence

- Ethical challenges of AI
- Bias in algorithms
- Accountability and transparency
- Guidelines for ethical development

Chapter 7: Next Steps

- Resources for deepening
- Communities and forums
- Practical projects
- Certifications

Conclusion

The journey in Artificial Intelligence is exciting and constantly evolving. This book is just the beginning of a fascinating adventure into the world of AI with Python.

About the Author

Guide designed for technology enthusiasts and computer science students.

Chapter 1: Fundamentals of Artificial Intelligence

1.1 What is Artificial Intelligence?

Artificial Intelligence (AI) is a field of computer science dedicated to creating systems capable of performing tasks that would normally require human intelligence. Essentially, it seeks to develop machines and software that can:

- Learning from experiences
- Solve complex problems
- Making decisions
- Recognize patterns
- Understand and process language
- Adapting to new situations

Scientific Definition

In the academic field, AI can be defined as a computational system capable of:

- Perceive your environment
- Process information
- Take actions that maximize your chances of success

1.2 Brief History of Artificial Intelligence

Landmarks

1. **1940s-1950s**: Early Concepts

    o Alan Turing proposes the "Turing Test"

    o Development of the first electronic computers

- o Beginning of discussions about "thinking" machines

2. **1950s-1960s**: Theoretical Foundation

   - o Dartmouth Conference (1956): Term "Artificial Intelligence" Coined

   - o Early AI Programs:

     - Logic Theorist

     - General Problem Solver

   - o Early optimism about AI's capabilities

3. **1970s-1980s**: First "AI Winter"

   - o Technological limitations

   - o Reduction of investments

   - o Criticism of initial expectations

4. **1990s–2000s**: Resurgence

   - o Increased computing power

   - o Development of more sophisticated algorithms

   - o Emergence of expert systems

5. **2010-present**: Deep Learning Revolution

   - o Deep Learning

   - o Advanced Neural Networks

   - o Natural Language Processing

   - o Generative AI

1.3 Types of Artificial Intelligence

1.3.1 Weak AI

- Focused on specific tasks

- Designed to solve well-defined problems
- Examples:
  - Virtual assistants
  - Recommendation systems
  - Image recognition

1.3.2 General AI (Strong AI)

- Human-like ability to understand and learn
- Adaptable to different contexts
- Still in the conceptual stage
- Objective: Replicate human intelligence in multiple areas

1.3.3 Superintelligent AI

- Hypothetical AI that surpasses human capabilities
- Ability to solve extremely complex problems
- Topic of ethical and philosophical discussions
- Present in scientific and science fiction debates

1.4 Fundamental Components of AI

Machine Learning

- Algorithms that enable systems to learn from data
- Types:
  - Supervised
  - Unsupervised
  - By reinforcement

Natural Language Processing (NLP)

- Ability to understand and generate human language
- Applications:
  - Translation
  - Chatbots
  - Sentiment analysis

Computer Vision

- Image and video interpretation
- Visual pattern recognition
- Applications in:
  - Safety
  - Medical diagnoses
  - Self-driving cars

1.5 Current Challenges of Artificial Intelligence

Technical Limitations

- Reliance on big data
- Bias in algorithms
- Explainability of models

Ethical Challenges

- Privacy
- Possible job replacement
- Potentially discriminatory algorithmic decisions

Future Perspectives

- Integration with other technologies

- More adaptive and contextual AI
- Focus on ethical and transparent solutions

Chapter Conclusion

Artificial Intelligence is not just a technology, but an ever-evolving field that promises to profoundly transform how we interact with computer systems and solve complex problems.

Key points for reflection:

- AI is a tool, not a universal solution
- Need for ethical development
- Importance of interdisciplinarity

Chapter 2: Setting Up the Development Environment for AI

2.1 Introduction to Environment Preparation

Setting up a robust development environment is crucial for any Artificial Intelligence project. This chapter will guide you through the essential steps to prepare your programming environment for AI projects using Python.

2.2 Python Installation

2.2.1 Installation Methods

1. **Direct Installation**
   - Download from the official website Python.org
   - Supports Windows, macOS, and Linux
   - Recommended for first-time users

2. **Anaconda (Recommended Distribution)**
   - Complete suite for data scientists
   - Includes Python and pre-installed scientific libraries

- o   Management of virtual environments made easy

Installation Verification Code

```python
python
import sys

# Checking Python version
print(f"Python version: {sys.version}")

# Checking installation pathprint(f"Python location: {sys.executable}")
```

2.3 Virtual Environments

Why use virtual environments?

- Dependency isolation

- Library version management

- Avoid conflicts between projects

Creation of Virtual Environment

Using venv

```bash
bash
# Creating python virtual environment
-m venv ia_env

# Activation on Windows
ia_env\Scripts\activate

# Activation on macOS/Linux
source ia_env/bin/activate
```

Using Conda

```bash
# Creating environment conda
conda create -n ia_ambiente python=3.9

# Enabling environment conda activate ia_ambiente
```

2.4 Development Tools

2.4.1 Recommended IDEs

1. **PyCharm**

   o Complete IDE for Python

   o Native support for AI development

   o Advanced debugging tools

2. **Visual Studio Code**

   o Lightweight and customizable

   o Extensions for AI and Machine Learning

   o Cross-platform support

3. **Jupyter Notebook**

   o Interactive environment

   o Ideal for data exploration

   o Integrated documentation

2.5 Essential Libraries for AI

Installation of Core Libraries

```bash
Bash
# Installation via pip
pip install numpy pandas scikit-learn tensorflow keras
matplotlib seaborn
```

Library Verification

```python
python
# Importing core libraries
import numpy as np
import pandas as pd
import sklearn
import tensorflow as tf
import matplotlib.pyplot as plt

# Checking versions
print(f"NumPy: {np.__version__}")print( f"Pandas:
{pd.__version__}")print(f"Scikit-learn:
{sklearn.__version__}")print(f"TensorFlow:
{tf.__version__}")
```

2.6 GPU Settings (Optional)

Facility for Deep Learning

```bash
bash
# TensorFlow installation with GPU support
pip install tensorflow-gpu
```

GPU Verification

```python
python
import tensorflow as tf

# Checking available GPUs
print("Available GPUs: ")
print(tf.config.list_physical_devices('GPU'))
```

2.7 Package Management

Creating requirements.txt

```bash
bash# Generating list of installed pip
 freeze packages  > requirements.txt

# Installing packages from a requirements
pip install -r requirements.txt
```

2.8 Good Configuration Practices

Important Tips

1. Keep Python and libraries up to date

2. Use virtual environments for each project

3. Document your settings

4. Back up regularly

5. Learn how to use version control (Git)

2.9 Troubleshooting Common Problems

Frequent Mistakes

- Version conflicts

- Library installation issues

- System incompatibilities

Support Resources

- Official documentation

- Community Forums

- Stack Overflow

- AI Discussion Groups

Chapter Conclusion

Setting up your development environment correctly is the crucial first step in your AI journey. Take the time to understand each tool and its settings.

Next steps:

- Practice Installation

- Explore the tools

- Create your first AI project

Practical Challenge: Install all the mentioned tools and create a working virtual environment for AI projects.

Chapter 3: Machine Learning Fundamentals

3.1 Introduction to Machine Learning

Definition

Machine Learning is a subfield of Artificial Intelligence that allows computational systems to learn and improve from experiences without being explicitly programmed.

Fundamental Components

- **Data**: Learning Raw Material

- **Algorithms**: Processing methods

- **Models**: Representations of learned patterns

3.2 Types of Machine Learning

3.2.1 Supervised Learning

Concept

- Algorithm trains with labeled data

- Objective: Predict outcomes for new data

Types of Problems

1. **Classification**
   - Predict categories
   - Example: Spam or non-spam

2. **Regression**
   - Predict numeric values
   - Example: House prices

Practical Example: Classification of Iris Flowers

```Python
from sklearn.datasets import load_iris

from sklearn.model_selection import train_test_split

from sklearn.preprocessing import StandardScaler

from sklearn.neighbors import KNeighborsClassifier

from sklearn.metrics import accuracy_score,
classification_report


# Loading dataset

iris = load_iris()

X, y = iris.data, iris.target


# Splitting data
```

```
X_treino, X_teste, y_treino, y_teste =
train_test_split(X, y, test_size=0.3, random_state=42)


# Normalizing data

scaler = StandardScaler()

X_treino_scaled = scaler.fit_transform(X_treino)

X_teste_scaled = scaler.transform(X_teste)


# Training classifier

classifier = KNeighborsClassifier(n_neighbors=3)

sorter.fit(X_treino_scaled, y_treino)


# Predicting outcomes

predictions = classifier.predict(X_teste_scaled)


# Evaluating model

print("Accuracy:", accuracy_score(y_teste, predictions))

print("\nRating Report:\n",
classification_report(y_teste, predictions))
```

3.2.2 Unsupervised Learning

Concept

- Works with unlabeled data

- Objective: To uncover hidden patterns

Types of Algorithms

1. **Clustering**
   - Group similar data
   - Example: Customer segmentation

2. **Dimensionality Reduction**
   - Simplify complex data
   - Example: Principal Component Analysis

Practical Example: K-Means Clustering

```python
from sklearn.datasets import load_iris
from sklearn.cluster import KMeans
import matplotlib.pyplot as plt

# Loading data
iris = load_iris()X = iris.data

# Applying K-Means
kmeans = KMeans(n_clusters=3, random_state=42)
kmeans.fit(X)

# Viewing clusters
plt.scatter(X[:, 0], X[:, 1], c=kmeans.labels_,
cmap='viridis')
plt.title('Clustering of Iris Flowers')
plt.xlabel('Sepal Length')
plt.ylabel('Sepal Width')
plt.show()
```

3.2.3 Reinforcement Learning

Concept

- Learning through interaction with the environment
- Based on rewards and punishments
- Common in games and robotics

Components

- **Agent**: System that learns
- **Environment**: Learning context
- **Actions**: Agent Decisions
- **Rewards**: Feedback from the environment

Simplified Q-Learning Example

```python
import numpy as np

class SimpleEnvironment: def __init__(self): self.states
= 6
self.actions =
2   self.q_table = np.zeros((self.states, self.actions))
def escolher_acao(self, state, epsilon=0.1): if
np.random.uniform(0, 1) < epsilon:
return np.random.choice(self.actions)
else: return np.argmax(self.q_table[state]) def
atualizar_q_table(self, state, action, reward,
proximo_estado, taxa_aprendizado=0.1,
fator_desconto=0.9): current = self.q_table[state,
action] maximo_futuro =
np.max(self.q_table[proximo_estado]) novo_valor = current
+ taxa_aprendizado * (reward + fator_desconto *
maximo_futuro - current) self.q_table[state, action] =
novo_valor

# Simplified training exampleenvironment =
```

```
SimpleEnvironment()
for episode in range(1000): state = np.random.randint(0,
environment.states) end = False
    while not end:
action = ambiente.escolher_acao(state) # Transition and
reward logic would be implemented here
 state = np.random.randint(0, environment.states) if
np.random.random() < 0.1: end = True

print("Resultant Q-Table:")print(ambiente.q_table)
```

3.3 Model Evaluation Metrics

Classification

- Accuracy
- Precision
- Recall
- F1-Score

Regression

- Mean Square Error (MSE)
- Mean Absolute Error (MAE)
- R-Squared

3.4 Challenges and Considerations

Common Issues

- Overfitting
- Underfitting
- Data bias
- Data quality

Good Practices

- Proper data division
- Cross-validation
- Normalization
- Missing data handling

Conclusion

Machine learning is a dynamic and powerful area that enables computer systems to learn from data, turning information into useful knowledge and accurate predictions.

Next steps:

- Practice with different datasets
- Experiment with multiple algorithms
- Study real-world use cases

Practical Challenge: Implement and compare different Machine Learning algorithms in the Iris dataset.

Chapter 4: Neural Networks and Deep Learning

4.1 Fundamentals of Neural Networks

4.1.1 Biological inspiration

Artificial neural networks are inspired by the functioning of the human brain:

- Biological neurons → Artificial neurons
- Synapses → Weighted Connections
- Nerve Impulses → Mathematical Signals

4.1.2 Basic Structure of an Artificial Neuron

1. **Inputs**

- o Input Data
- o Each entry has an associated weight

2. **Activation Function**
   - o Transforms the weighted sum of the inputs
   - o Decides whether the neuron "fires"
   - o Common types:
     - Sigmoid
     - ReLU (Rectified Linear Unit)
     - Tanh

Example of Artificial Neuron

```python
import numpy as np

class Neuron: def __init__(self): # Randomly initialized
weights
self.weights = np.random.rand(3) self.bias =
np.random.rand() def funcao_ativacao_sigmoid(self, x):
return 1 / (1 + np.exp(-x)) def forward(self, inputs): #
Weighted sum of inputs
 sum = np.dot(inputs, self.weights) + self.bias #
Applying activation function
return self.funcao_ativacao_sigmoid(sum)

# Example of use
neuron = Neuron() inputs = np.array([1.0, 2.0, 3.0])
output = neuron.forward(inputs) print("Neuron output:",
output)
```

4.2 Neural Network Architecture

4.2.1 Types of Layers

1. **Input Layer**

   o   Receives original data

   o   Number of neurons = number of features

2. **Hidden Layers**

   o   Process information

   o   Can have multiple layers

   o   Increase model complexity

3. **Output Layer**

   o   Produces final result

   o   Format depends on the problem (classification/regression)

4.2.2 Types of Neural Networks

1. **Multi-Layer Perceptron (MLP)**

2. **Convolutional Networks (CNN)**

3. **Recurring Networks (RNN)**

4. **Transformers**

4.3 Simple Neural Network Implementation

```python
import numpy as np
import matplotlib.pyplot as plt
from sklearn.model_selection import train_test_split
from sklearn.datasets import make_classification
from sklearn.preprocessing import StandardScaler

class NeuralNetwork: def __init__(self,
```

```python
camadas_neuronios): self.layers = len(camadas_neuronios)
self.weights = [] self.bias = [] # Initializing weights
and bias  for
 i in range(1, len(camadas_neuronios)):
self.weights.append(np.random.randn(camadas_neuronios[i-
1], camadas_neuronios[i]))
self.bias.append(np.random.randn(camadas_neuronios[i]))
def sigmoid(self, x): return 1 / (1 + np.exp(-x)) def
sigmoid_derivada(self, x): return x * (1 - x) def
train(self, X, y, epochs=10000, taxa_aprendizado=0.1):
for _ in range(epochs): # Feedforward
camada_ativacao = [X] for i in range(self.layers - 1):
proxima_camada = np.dot(camada_ativacao[-1],
self.weights[i]) + self.bias[i]
camada_ativacao.append(self.sigmoid(proxima_camada)) #
Backpropagation
 error = y - camada_ativacao[-1] deltas = [error *
self.sigmoid_derivada(camada_ativacao[-1])] for i in
range(self.layers - 2, 0, -1): erro_camada = deltas[-
1].dot(self.weights[i]. T) delta = erro_camada *
self.sigmoid_derivada(camada_ativacao[i])
deltas.append(delta) deltas.reverse() # Weights update
for i in range(self.layers - 1):
                self.weights[i] += taxa_aprendizado *
np.dot(camada_ativacao[i]. T, deltas[i])  self.bias[i] +=
taxa_aprendizado * np.sum(deltas[i], axis=0) def
predict(self, X): camada_ativacao = X for i in
range(self.layers - 1): camada_ativacao =
self.sigmoid(np.dot(camada_ativacao, self.weights[i]) +
self.bias[i])  return camada_ativacao


# Data preparationX, y =
make_classification(n_samples=1000, n_features=20,
n_classes=2, random_state=42)
X_treino, X_teste, y_treino, y_teste =
train_test_split(X, y, test_size=0element.2)
```

```python
# Scaler Normalization
= StandardScaler()
X_treino = scaler.fit_transform(X_treino)
X_teste = scaler.transform(X_teste)

# Network Configuration and Training
Network = NeuralNetwork([20, 10, 5, 1])
network.train(X_treino, y_treino.reshape(-1, 1))

#
Predictions predictions = network.predict(X_teste)
accuracy = np.mean((predictions > 0.5) ==
y_teste)print(f"Model Accuracy: {accuracy * 100:.2f}%")
```

4.4 Deep Learning with TensorFlow/Keras

```python
python
import tensorflow as tffrom tensorflow.keras.models
import Sequentialfrom tensorflow.keras.layers import
Densefrom tensorflow.keras.optimizers import Adam

# Model configuration
= Sequential([ Dense(64, activation='relu',
input_shape=(20,)),
 Dense(32, activation='relu'),
 Dense(16, activation='relu'),
 Dense(1, activation='sigmoid')
])#

# Model
compilation.compile( optimizer=Adam(learning_rate=0.001),
loss='binary_crossentropy', metrics=['accuracy']


)
```

```
# Historical training
 = model.fit( X_treino, y_treino, validation_split=0.2,
epochs=50, batch_size=32

)

# Evaluation
result = model.evaluate(X_teste, y_teste)print("Accuracy
in test set:", result[1])
```

4.5 Challenges in Neural Networks

Common Issues

1. Overfitting
2. Vanishing Gradient
3. Hyperparameter choice
4. Need for big data

Mitigation Techniques

- Regularisation
- Dropout
- Batch Normalization
- Transfer learning

4.6 Practical Applications

Application Areas

- Image Recognition
- Natural Language Processing
- Time Series Forecasting
- Medical Diagnostics

- Games and Robotics

Conclusion

Neural Networks and Deep Learning represent the state of the art in Artificial Intelligence, allowing computer systems to learn complex representations from data.

Next steps:

- Experiment with different architectures
- Participate in ML competitions
- Study advanced use cases

Practical Challenge: Implement a neural network for a specific classification or regression problem.

Chapter 5: Natural Language Processing (NLP)

Definition and Fundamental Concepts

Natural Language Processing (NLP) is a subfield of artificial intelligence that focuses on the interaction between computers and human language. Its main purpose is to allow machines to understand, interpret, and generate text or speech in a similar way to humans.

Key Components of NLP

1. **Linguistic Analysis**
   - Tokenization
   - Morphological analysis
   - Syntactic Parsing
   - Semantic analysis

2. **Fundamental Techniques**
   - Stemming

- o Stemming
- o Recognition of named entities
- o Sentiment analysis

Practical Applications of NLP

Word Processing

- Machine translation
- Text generation
- Document Summarization
- Chatbots and virtual assistants

Data Analysis

- Information extraction
- Document classification
- Opinion mining
- Social media sentiment analysis

Challenges in NLP

1. **Linguistic Ambiguity**
   - o Words with multiple meanings
   - o Contextual interpretation
   - o Grammatical and regional variations

2. **Computational Complexities**
   - o Processing languages with complex structures
   - o Dealing with slang and informal expressions
   - o Interpretation of semantic nuances

Modern Technologies and Tools

Python Libraries

- NLTK (Natural Language Toolkit)

- spaCy

- Gensim

- Transformers (Hugging Face)

Language Models

- Word Embeddings

- Recurrent Neural Networks (RNN)

- Transformers

- BERT

- GPT

Practical Example of Word Processing

```python
import nltk
from nltk.tokenize import word_tokenize
from nltk.sentiment import SentimentIntensityAnalyzer

# Example texttext = "I'm very happy with the results of
the project!"

# Tokenizationtokens = word_tokenize(text)

# Sentiment Analysis =
SentimentIntensityAnalyzer()sentiment =
sia.polarity_scores(text)
```

Future Trends in NLP

1. More accurate language models

2. Multimodal machine learning

3. More contextual and adaptable NLP

4. Real-time translation with greater accuracy

5. More sophisticated virtual assistants

Ethical Considerations

- Bias in language models

- Data privacy

- Algorithmic transparency

- Social impact of NLP technologies

Conclusion

Natural Language Processing represents a fascinating frontier of artificial intelligence, enabling increasingly natural interactions between humans and machines.

Chapter 6: Ethics in Artificial Intelligence

1. Ethical Foundations of AI

Fundamental Principles

- AI ethics involves ensuring that artificial intelligence systems are developed and used responsibly and beneficially for society

- It seeks to balance technological potential with moral and humanitarian considerations

- Considers the long-term impacts of AI technologies on individuals and communities

2. Main Ethical Challenges

Bias and Discrimination

- AI systems can perpetuate or amplify existing biases
- Need for development of fair and impartial algorithms
- Importance of diversity in development teams to mitigate bias

Privacy and Data Protection

- Protection of personal data used in AI training
- Informed consent and transparency in the use of information
- Regulations such as LGPD and GDPR as important legal frameworks

Transparency and Applicability

- Development of understandable and interpretable AI systems
- Ability to explain decisions made by algorithms
- Combating the "black box" of machine learning systems

3. Ethical Responsibility

Developers' Responsibility

- Ethical commitment in the development of technologies
- Consideration of social and individual impacts
- Creating guidelines and codes of conduct for AI professionals

Governance and Regulation

- Need for AI-specific regulatory frameworks
- Collaboration between public, private and academic sectors
- Development of international AI ethics standards

4. Emerging Moral Dilemmas

Autonomy and Decision Making

- Limits of autonomy of AI systems
- Questions about decisions in critical areas (health, justice, security)
- Maintaining human control in automated systems

Impact on the Labor Market

- Transformations in labor relations
- Need for transition and reskilling policies
- Equitable distribution of automation benefits

5. Future Prospects

Proactive Ethical Development

- Integration of ethical considerations from the earliest stages of development
- Continuing Education in Ethics for Technology Professionals
- Multidisciplinary approach involving specialists in different areas

Guiding Principles

- Respect for human rights
- Promotion of social welfare
- Precaution and responsibility
- Transparency and accountability

Conclusion

AI ethics is not a secondary topic, but a key component in ensuring that technology truly serves human interests, promoting progress with responsibility and respect.

Chapter 7: Next Steps in Artificial Intelligence

1. Resources for Deepening

Online Learning Platforms

- **Coursera**
  - Courses from renowned universities
  - Specialization in Machine Learning (Stanford)
  - AI Professional Certificates
- **edX**
  - Courses from MIT, Harvard
  - Advanced programs in AI and Machine Learning
- **Udacity**
  - Nanodegrees in AI
  - Practical training with real projects
  - Partnerships with technology companies

Libraries and Frameworks

- **Python**
  - TensorFlow
  - PyTorch
  - Scikit-learn
  - Keras
- **Open Source Resources**
  - GitHub
  - Kaggle
  - Google Colab

2. Communities and Forums

Online Communities

- **Reddit**
  - r/MachineLearning
  - r/artificial
  - r/DataScience
- **Discord**
  - Specialized AI servers
  - Interactive study groups
- **Stack Overflow**
  - Technical support
  - Specific troubleshooting

Professional Groups

- **LinkedIn Groups**
  - Artificial Intelligence Professionals
  - Machine Learning Community
- **Scientific Associations**
  - IEEE Computer Society
  - ACM SIGAI (Special Interest Group on Artificial Intelligence)

3. Practical Projects

Development Areas

- **Natural Language Processing**
  - Chatbots
  - Translation systems

- o Sentiment analysis
- **Computer Vision**
  - o Facial recognition
  - o Object detection
  - o Security systems
- **Data Analysis**
  - o Trend forecasting
  - o Recommendation systems
  - o Predictive analytics

Platforms for Projects

- **Kaggle**
  - o AI Competitions
  - o Public datasets
  - o Development environment
- **GitHub**
  - o Project repositories
  - o Open-source collaboration
  - o Professional portfolio

4. Professional Certifications

Technical Certifications

- **Google**
  - o Google Professional Machine Learning Engineer
  - o TensorFlow Developer Certificate

- **Microsoft**
  - Azure AI Engineer
  - Microsoft Certified: AI Engineer Associate
- **AWS**
  - AWS Certified Machine Learning - Specialty
  - AWS Deep Learning Certification

Academic Certifications

- **IBM**
  - IBM Data Science Professional Certificate
  - IBM AI Engineering Professional Certificate
- **Stanford Online**
  - Certificate in AI
  - Machine Learning Extension Program

5. Professional Development Strategies

Tips for Growth

- Develop a consistent portfolio
- Participate in hackathons
- Contribute to open-source projects
- Stay up-to-date with scientific publications
- Networking with professionals in the field

Emerging Areas

- Generative AI
- Ethical Learning

- Explainable AI

- Sustainable Artificial Intelligence

Conclusion

The field of Artificial Intelligence is constantly evolving. Continuous learning, hands-on practice, and community connection are key to professional success.

Author

 Paulo Fagundes is an information technology professional with senior experience in Artificial Intelligence and Software Development. He has a solid background in programming logic and machine learning, having worked on several projects that combine technological innovation and practical solutions.

Currently, Paulo is Chief AI Officer (CAIO) at MakeAI Innovations, where he leads artificial intelligence development initiatives. He also serves as GenAI/Security Prompt Lead Engineer, AI Research Scientist, Machine Learning Master Engineer, and Data Engineer. In addition, he owns the CodeXpert AI profiles on X and Instagram, where he shares insights and resources on programming and AI.

Passionate about teaching and sharing knowledge, Paulo is always looking for new ways to demystify complex concepts, making them accessible to everyone. He believes that education is the key to the future, especially in the area of technology, where adaptation and continuous learning are essential.

You can connect with Paulo and follow his work through his LinkedIn profile: Paulo Fagundes